JOURNEY FROM DARKNESS TO
LIGHT

BUBBY WALLACE

Copyright © 2021 by Bubby Wallace

All rights reserved, including the right to reproduce this book or portions thereof in any form whatsoever or by any means. No part of this book may be reproduced, stored in a retrieval system, or transmitted by any means without the written permission of the author, except as provided by United States of America copyright law.

First Paperback edition October, 2021

Manufactured in the United States of America

Scriptures referred to in this book are taken from the most up to date translations of the Holy Bible published by Zondervan Publishing House and provided online by biblegateway.com.

Many names have been changed to protect their identity.

Published by Victory Vision
Publishing and Consulting
victoryvision.org

ISBN: 9798481817927

DEDICATION

This book is dedicated to those who may be struggling with addiction and who desire to believe in Jesus.

CONTENTS

	Acknowledgments	i
	Endorsements	iii
	Introduction	v
1	The Light of Life	1
2	The Beginning of Darkness	15
3	The Diminishing of Light	29
4	Deep Darkness	43
5	More Bad Choices	55
6	Rock Bottom	63
7	Jesus, The Light of My Life	75
8	Recovering from the Darkness	87
9	Living in the Light	93
	About the Author	111

ACKNOWLEDGMENTS

I would like to thank my wife, Elaine, and friend, Debbie Shoemaker, for their prayers and support in getting this book to the Publisher.

ENDORSEMENT

"I was impressed when I read 'JOURNEY FROM DARKNESS TO LIGHT!' by a young hearted and passionate man of God, Bubby Wallace. As a fellow author and close friend, this book moved me with its practical and personal insights that teach men and women about how you can overcome your past and live a better future. Bubby has unfolded a powerful revelation that provides his readers with specific steps they can take to find happiness within and achieve success through a relationship with the Lord. I recommend obtaining a copy of this book to add to your bookshelf because it's filled with useful information that every person struggling with pride should know."

~ Ron Smith
Author, Substance Abuse Professional, and owner of Delivered2Choices Outpatient Treatment Program.

INTRODUCTION

As a young man, I made a bad decision for my life: I decided I wanted to do life my way. I wanted to be free to do whatever I wanted, not allowing anyone, no matter who they were, to tell me what to do. This decision caused me to live half of my life in darkness, not understanding how the consequences of my choices were damaging me mentally, emotionally, and most damaging of all, spiritually. Consequently, this decision brought me many years of addiction, dysfunctional relationships, homelessness, jail time, mental hospitals, and spiritual darkness.

Let me assure you, all my bad choices came with bad results. They either brought harm to those around me or pain and suffering in my own life. Then one day after many years of doing whatever I wanted, I realized that my life was a horrible mess.

I was tired of the damage I had done to myself, as well as to my family. I knew that the only one that could help me now was God, so I cried out for help, and He came to my rescue. After thirty years of living in darkness, I finally made a solid choice to allow the Light of the world, Jesus Christ, into my life. This is the story of how Jesus saved me from the darkness that wanted to destroy me and gave me the Light of life that I might walk in a brand-new way.

"This is the message we have heard from him and declare to you: God is light; in him there is no darkness at all. If we claim to have fellowship with him and yet walk in the darkness, we lie and do not live out the truth. But if we walk in the light, as he is in the light, we have fellowship with one another, and the blood of Jesus, his Son, purifies us from all sin." (1 John 1:5-7 {NIV})

CHAPTER 1: THE LIGHT OF LIFE

I was born February 23, 1960, in Sacramento, California. In fact, I have lived here most all my life. I grew up on the north side of town, right in between what a lot of people would call 'the worst parts of Sacramento.' As I grew up, I learned a great deal from both sides of the city. Mostly, I learned the things that got me into a lot of trouble later in my life. I was one of the middle children in the family of eight kids my mom bore to my dad. As a child, everything in my life seemed normal. Family and friends were always a joy to be around; I can remember only good times whenever we came together. All the holidays from my childhood bring back great memories of how a normal life in America used to be.

Dad was from Alabama, and Mom was from Oklahoma. We did not have much money, and we moved often. However, we did not ever move a great distance. I believe I went to six different elementary schools before I made it to my only jr. high school in Rio Linda, California. We did move two different times to Gold Hill, Oregon. My grandparents had moved there sometime in the 1960s, moving in next door to my grandmother's sister because my grandfather was diagnosed with lung cancer. He had contracted the cancer from asbestos while working in the rail yards in downtown Sacramento. The doctors said he would live longer up there in the cleaner air.

I remember we tried to settle in Gold Hill twice. Once in 1965-66, when I was in the first grade, and then again in 1969-70, when I was in the fifth grade. It was a very small town and my brothers, sisters, and I loved it. We attended a small Assembly of God church there, and we had a great time being a part of that little church and community. It was there in Oregon where I first experienced the amazing supernatural power of God. That same supernatural power of God would later deliver me from the evil and wickedness that would consume my life beyond anything I could ever have imagined.

I went to Patrick Elementary school in Gold Hill. I was the only fifth grader who made the junior varsity football team. In Oregon at that time, elementary school was for children in first grade to fifth grade and middle school was for sixth, seventh and eighth graders. It was exciting for me because, unlike the schools in California where I spent most of my school years, in Oregon we got to play tackle football with complete uniforms. Not only did I make the team, but somehow, I made first string halfback. I was quite small, fast, and difficult to tackle, and these attributes were the first sign of any talent that I can remember. I did not do well in school when it came to grades, but I had some skills when it came to sports!

By the time I made it into junior high, I had sprouted into a handsome, athletic young man.

Around that time, I started realizing that the cute girls in school liked me and that the talented boys from the basketball team wanted me on their team. However, all that attention made my pride grow like Miracle-Gro on tomato plants, causing my life to begin to really change. It was about this time in my life that I wanted to be free from any authority over me. Most of my friends were older than me, and it seemed to me that they got to do whatever they wanted

without getting into trouble with their parents. So that is how I started living my life; I began doing whatever I wanted. I stopped coming home and stopped going to school. I started living in the streets, doing drugs, drinking, popping pills, and having sex with any girl that would let me.

Here is what you need to know: I did not leave home because of the problems that were going on in the home. I left because I wanted to be free of authority; I did not want anyone telling me what to do. I felt this would make me happiest, but eventually that attitude caused many, many problems in my life.

For the most part, I hung out in my old neighborhood. It was only a few miles down the road to our new house. It was not like I was a long way from home; however, it was at this time that my parents were no longer able to keep me at home or in school. My dad mostly worked and hung out with his fishing and drinking buddies, and at about that time, my mom was busy with a new baby. So, I decided I did not want to be at home anymore. Though my mom wanted me there, her best efforts could not keep me at home.

My mom still somehow managed to keep in contact with me. She was able to get me to come home on occasion, but I never stayed long. Being so independent, I was determined to be on my own. I was doing everything the 'grownups' were doing in those days, adult things like smoking cigarettes. Because my mom could not keep me from taking her cigarettes, she reluctantly started giving them to me, and I could tell it was something that she really did not want to do.

Right before my mom realized she was pregnant with her eighth child, she thought she was dying of some illness. This was the first time that I can remember mom ever speaking about Heaven and Jesus. She started telling us kids about how the Bible described Heaven. She would say the streets are paved in gold. She also said you will never die, but you will live forever with Jesus. Those might not be the exact words, but she was extremely passionate about her interest in the Bible and what it was saying about Heaven at that time. This was also about the time my mom started realizing that her husband and my father was not all she had hoped he would be. After she caught him with other women, something inside her began to change.

Even though I was in the streets running wild and out of control, life went on for my family at home. I would often stay at the homes of different friends, just whoever would let me hang out. I was not a lazy kid; I would help with whatever they might ask me to do. Some of my friends had farms, some owned wrecking yards, and some of them had two working parents. My favorite place to stay was at my Italian friend's home. At their home, there was the father, Jim, and his three sons, Jim Jr., Fred, and Richie. When I would stay there, they would really take care of me. Jim Sr. was a carpenter by trade, but he was getting old. Eventually, he took a janitor's job at a school. Jim Jr. and Richie attended school, but Fred and I stayed home and would help Jim Sr. however we could. When he had places to go, he would let us drive him around in his old Chevy truck or his station wagon. Being so young, I thought it was a lot of fun to be able to do grown up things.

One of the things I learned about Sicilians is you do not want to mess with their family, or those they considered true friends. All three of the sons knew how to fight. One evening, Jim Jr., Fred, and I got into a street brawl with some grownups in the neighborhood. This changed my perspective about true friends. It was unreal how these older guys wanted to hurt us. We were just neighborhood kids with long hair. This was my first street brawl, and it scared me to death. I ran home to their house while they fought off these adult men. Believe it or not, those boys beat those grown men very badly. Jim Sr. scolded me for running and leaving his boys to deal with all that themselves. He told me, next time you must pick up something to help, like a bat or pic handle, but do not ever run from a fight again!

After that, they put the boxing gloves on me and taught me how to box. There was no more running from fights. In fact, I became rather good at it, even liking it when a fight came my way. We never really went looking for fights, but if you challenged us in any way, you would have a fight on your hands. Today, two of those brothers are still alive. Throughout the years, we have always been there for each other. Fred and I were the closest. He was like a big brother that protected me, always looking out for me. He is in Heaven now. I found out at his funeral that he had given his life to the Lord. It is awesome to know that I will see my buddy in Heaven.

I remember my first paying job as a kid. I was a parts puller at a wrecking yard. I was probably fourteen years old at the time. It was a lot of fun because I got to drive the yard cars and drink beer occasionally, as well as make money to buy my own cigarettes. At that time, I was living with Jesse, one of the sons of the owner of the wrecking yard. This was when I met my first love, Rachel. I have to say that she was blonde and beautiful, and I fell head over heels for her. With great intensity, Rachel told me that she would always love me. Of course, we had no idea what love truly was. It was not until she broke up with me six months later that I realized I really did love her; that I had allowed her into my heart. By that time, I was living in the streets, and I had just found out my family had packed up and moved. I guess my dad had gotten a job for himself and one of my older brothers with a logging company doing helicopter logging.

So, there I was, brokenhearted, and it was no joke. I had no idea that such pain existed in the world; I was completely devastated. I cannot tell you if my friends or anyone else knew the pain I was in. All I know is, I kept it inside and do not remember talking with anyone about what was happening inside my heart or how I was feeling. In fact, I did not understand it myself, so I did not know how to tell anyone. I think I believed that old lie, the one that says men are supposed to suck it up because you are a man, and just move on. I just thought that is how it is supposed to be, so ultimately, that is just what I did.

My oldest brother, Dean, had just gotten out of the Air Force and was living across town. I made my way to his house, and Dean and his family let me stay there until my dad finally came and got me. Dad took me back to the campground they were living right next to the Trinity River. When I showed up at the campground, I knew my mom had one less worry. I know now that she wanted to leave my dad and be done with all the stress that came with being married to an angry drunk who could not be the loving husband or father she had hoped he would be. As the summer ended, my mom had grown tired of camping and told my dad he needed to get us a home.

So, they found a house out in the cattle lands in Red Bluff, California. My dad continued to travel with the logging company, while we lived out in the boonies with a bunch of rednecks. It was a small housing complex that consisted of mostly low-income people with family issues, life issues, substance abuse issues, and drinking issues. I am sorry to say I was in the middle of all of them. In fact, a few of my friends and I were sometimes the problem in that neighborhood. All of us kids in the neighborhood were learning how to drink, smoke pot, and chew or smoke tobacco. I believe I was around fifteen years old, and I had long hair and hung out with all the wrong people. Red Bluff was the place I got my ear pierced, got my first tattoo, and surprisingly, got my friend Mark's sister pregnant.

Lori was older than me and had pursued me. She would lie to her parents, telling them she was going to church with my mom, but would stay home with me instead. Then

Journey from Darkness to Light

one day when my dad was on break from logging, her dad showed up at our house. Apparently, Lori had used the public school system to obtain an abortion without her parents' consent. Completely oblivious, I had no idea until my dad approached me about the situation. As the story goes, they had sent her to some clinic to have the procedure; during the process, one of the nurses had left Lori alone in the recovery room way too long, and she had almost bled to death. Her parents were extremely angry with the school, which really made my part insignificant to the whole sad and bad situation. I have a child I never had a chance to meet, but I will when I make it to Heaven. Not long after the abortion, Lori turned eighteen. Because I was only fifteen at the time, nothing ever came toward me and my part in that tragedy. The family moved out of the neighborhood soon after, and it was not long after they left that my family moved back to Sacramento.

Before we moved from Red Bluff, my dad went off to work somewhere with the logging company. This was the opportunity my mom had been waiting for; she had decided it was time to leave my dad. Quickly, she found us a place back in Sacramento, so we packed our stuff and got out of there as fast as we could. I do not think she told us or anyone else exactly where we were going, but it really felt like we were starting a new life. We found a lot of peace in our home without our alcoholic dad in it.

# CHAPTER 2: THE BEGINNING OF DARKNESS

We landed in North Highlands, a suburb of Sacramento. It was around 1975-76. I was a little familiar with our new neighborhood, as one of my oldest and best friends, Sean, lived on the outskirts of North Highlands. When I was growing up, I used to visit him fairly often. Now Sean's buddies from school became my buddies in no time. My friend, Sean, found out I was living on their side of town.

At this time in my life, I became awfully familiar with practicing bad habits, including addictive behaviors. In fact, my adolescent days were filled with learning how to be a hoodlum and a knucklehead. When I was between the ages of sixteen and nineteen, the people I hung around with just wanted to party and have fun. And that is exactly what we did! Everything we did centered around drinking, doing drugs, and having sex. Yes, it was the seventies, and these things were happening everywhere I turned.

Some of our friends went to school, and through them we would find out where there was going to be a party, or we would have one ourselves. It usually consisted of a keg of beer and a bunch of high school kids. Before the night was over, we would usually end up fighting with someone about something stupid. Living that way in those days, the bad ways and habits of life started developing in me, and eventually, these led to a vicious cycle of jail time and mental institutions.

After we moved back to the Sacramento area, a couple of years had passed when I met the girl who would become my first wife. Lacey was working at an A&W restaurant where they still came out to the car to serve you, though not on roller-skates like in the fifties and sixties. I met her through my cousin Rhonda who had gotten a job there. Lacey really wanted to settle down and start a family; however, I was still wild and out of control. Our relationship had been off and on for about a year when Lacey found out she was pregnant.

After that, some of our friends talked us into getting married, so she moved in with me and my family as I tried to do the right thing. I started by getting a job at a construction company. Sadly, it was not long after we started our life together that Lacey lost the baby. We eventually got our own place, and she got a good job.

It was not long after that I went back to my old ways, and after about a year of my foolishness, Lacey told me that she was pregnant again, and that she was going home to her mom's. She soon gave birth to a healthy little boy, Paul. She did not really try to make me be responsible as a dad or husband; instead, she just went her way, and I went mine.

Like any bad habit, I went back to hanging out with my old buddies in all the wrong places. It was not long after being back in the mix of it all that I met the girl who would be my second wife, Diane. She was just becoming part of the click that I hung out with; not only that, Diane was just my type: blonde; beautiful; and she loved to do all the things I liked to do. We instantly fell in love and went everywhere together. However, I do not think that either of us were in a hurry to share our new relationship with our parents. I was way too out of control for her parents, and it was too soon after my first marriage for me to bring her around mine.

One sunny hot summer Saturday, while my Diane was at work, I went out with a bunch of my friends to party at a local lake. Of course, we were all drinking, and we met two off duty airmen from a local Air Force base. It just so happened that they were partying right next to us, and when they came over to us, they began getting arrogant towards us. They were also being too friendly with the girls we had with us. Well, it was not long until push came to

shove, and we fought. Unfortunately, one of our guys took the airmen's wallets and stole their money. Someone called the police, and we got pulled over as we were on our way out. Some of us got arrested right away and some of us got arrested later.

We soon faced our day in court, and sadly enough for us, the judge of the little town where we went to court was up for re-election. Looking to find renewed favor with the voters, he was passing out big jail sentences in hopes of being re-elected. Long story short, some of us went to prison, and some of us got lots of county jail time. Me? I got a yearlong sentence in the county jail. This was not my first time in jail, but it was the first time I would spend more than a few weeks or months there.

Unfortunately, my eight months in the county jail did not change me for the better in any way. While I was locked up, I did what I had always done; I hung out with the older crowd and learned how to be a better bad person, if there is such a thing. It just seemed like I was really good at doing the wrong things in life.

I got lucky and was put on the honor side of the jail which were some old army barracks a few miles away from the main jail. An older guy that I really got along with taught me how to lift weights and get really fit. Of course, all that did was expand my selfish, self-centered, and prideful ways beyond measure.

The first night I was out, I went to a party which was being thrown for me. The same old thing happened again: my buddies and I got drunk and got into a fight. While I was there, I was trying to reunite with Lacey. As a matter of fact, I had brought her to the party. After seeing Diane at the party, however, she and I spoke in secret, and we realized that were still in love with each other!

Diane and I continued to date, and eventually we moved in together. We started slowly allowing our parents into the relationship and life seemed good to me, mostly because one of us had a really good job...and it was not me. Through one of our friends, she had gotten a job with a catering company, and she made good money. Me? I stayed home and did whatever my buddies and I wanted to do. Yet even though I did nothing to support us, we decided to have a baby, and that changed everything. Diane told me that I had to get a job or else! She kept working almost all the way through the pregnancy. She went right back to work after our son Garry was born, and I stayed home with him.

Eventually, I decided that I did need a good job, so I came up with this awesome plan. I decided that I wanted to go to trade school because I had friends who worked with heavy equipment, and it paid a lot of money. Of course, at that time life was all about the money, drinking, and man toys. Even though I had somehow made it through the six months of the book work at home., my plan fell through. The second part of the course was to be at a school in Southern California where I would get special training on the real equipment. As I proceeded to make plans to get to the school, I found out that it had closed, but not before a bunch of people had been scammed out of their money. This put a dead stop to my big plans. I was having a great time at home with Garry when my younger brother, Brent, got a job at a truss yard, and he told me I could probably get on there. So, I applied and was hired. It was a good job, and I loved it. Diane really loved it too because it appeared that I was finally taking some responsibility for our lives.

This job really opened the door with her parents, Mark and Ellie, and soon we started getting invited to their home. This was particularly good for me. Her folks just seemed to have it all together. First of all, Mark and Ellie owned their own home, and they had all kinds of toys that my family never seemed to be able to afford. They had nice cars, trucks, camping trailers, dirt bikes, street bikes and good jobs that paid well. My family had always lived from paycheck to paycheck as we kids were growing up. It seemed we had only enough to get by; there would never be enough for nice stuff or a nice home. In fact, when I was a kid there were times that my entire family would go out to the peach orchards to pick peaches during the summer, just so we could have school clothes. We never seemed to be able to get it together like Diane's family did. Her parents drank just like my dad, but they still did well for themselves.

Life seemed to be going well for us. I was loving my job and climbing the ladder quickly. I worked hard, and the guys that were there for a long time showed me favor.

I would eventually wind up with one of the best jobs at the truss yard. A guy named Al took me under his wing and taught me how to run the big saws there; he had been running one for years. Al soon got

promoted to a much easier job driving a forklift. So, because he had trained me, I became the new rafter saw operator. There were guys that had been there for years hoping to get a position like that in the yard. Believe me, they were not happy when the boss gave it to me; I had been there only two years.

Then about a year later, the owners decided to sell the place. It was somewhat heart breaking because I had been hoping to retire from there. Well, my brother-in-law Freddy worked for a carpet company and invited me to come fill out an application. He hung out with the guys that oversaw the warehouse, so he put in a good word for me, and I got the job. This was a time when my drinking escalated faster than any other time in my life.

For the three and half years at this job, we would start drinking beer by ten o'clock in the morning. We did this almost every day, and then we would hang and drink for a couple of more hours after work. Then I usually picked up a twelve-pack on my way home. At that time in my life, I thought it was a great job. I eventually became a favorite with the warehouse foremen because we all played golf together. The job paid very well, and it had great benefits for my family. I was once again hoping to spend enough time there to provide a good retirement for myself and my family.

One day, however, the foreman came out of the main office and told us that one of the owners was getting a divorce. Due to this event, they were closing the doors. This hit me hard, and I started thinking that I had some black cloud following me or something. They told us we had about three months until they closed the doors. Then the company offered all of us an opportunity to use their trucks to get our Class 'A' truck driver's licenses. Not only were they giving me a great opportunity to get my class 'A' license, but I was also invited to stick around for about three months to help one of the foremen pack up everything. We put all the inventory in truck trailers, then sent everything to the main warehouse in Oakland. Of course, we were getting paid, and most of the time we were the only two workers at the warehouse.

Though we were not slackers and did our jobs, the empty office meant no bosses around, so we always had beer on hand. We stayed on course and got our work done, but we also drank. Yet, through it all, the work, and the drinking, I still somehow was able to study the DMV manual quickly and got my class 'A' permit. Eventually, I went and took the driving test and passed.

Getting my class 'A' license was a big deal to me because it meant a good job with good pay and medical benefits for me and my family. It meant a lot to me because the jobs my dad got never seemed to completely provide for our family. For quite a few years, I appeared to most people as a functional drunk. However, had it not been for Diane's responsible ways during the thirteen years we were together, things probably would not have gone as well for us. Not that all of it was good during that time. I was verbally abusive, and I am sure if you were to ask her, a lot of that time was pure hell for her.

My two older brothers did not wind up like my dad; however, I did. For many years, everybody who knew both me and my dad would say, "Bubby, you're just like your dad." We were both hard-headed, foul-mouthed drunks. For most of my life, I was very opinionated and had horrible control issues. Not only that, I had a jealous spirit from hell. If anyone messed with me and my family, I was not afraid to convince them they had messed with the wrong person. Whether by fist or mouth, they were going to hear from me.

I am not bragging; it is what years of drinking, drugs and growing up in the streets did to me.

CHAPTER 3: THE DIMINISHING OF LIGHT

My dad was a truck driver for many years. He had been my hero for most of my life, and I wanted to be like just him, though I did want a better life than his. I wanted better things for my wife and kids. So, any time I could climb the workforce ladder, it meant the world to me; it meant I was becoming a responsible father who genuinely cared about his family. It meant I was doing better than the life I grew up in; it meant no more beans and potatoes five or six days a week.

Truth is, I loved my dad, and we were very close. We loved the same things most of our lives. He would give the shirt off his back for most of his friends. He loved to drink, fish, and hang out at bars; he also liked to go lots of places with his buddies. And yes, I did a lot of that starting out, but after Diane and I had kids, it was all about my immediate and close family. We did everything together; we, being my brothers and their families along with my wife and her family.

Everything seemed so right and so good, and that would have been my evaluation of things back then. However, it really was not; everyone else would have told you another story. To be honest, people feared me because of my jealousy and raging anger. These had developed in me mostly through drinking, using drugs, and growing up so hard.

Eventually, Diane could not take it anymore. She had finally had enough of my verbal abuse and got up the courage to leave me. I tried to be a tough guy at first and go on without her, but I finally concluded that I had lost everything that meant the most to me in life. The loss of my wife and kids devastated me beyond anything I had ever dealt with before. I desperately tried all my old tricks to get her back, but she was not buying any more of my fear-based manipulation. In the past, I had always done the same thing and coerced her to come back to me.

Nope. This time she was really done with me. She went home to her mom and dad, and I stayed in our home for a while. Eventually, I allowed my younger sister Brenda and her family to live with me. I was hurt and lonely and did not want to be alone in that house. This was a very hard time for me, and I had some serious emotional struggles that made me consider suicide. I once tried drinking and taking a bunch of pills, but more than anything, I just wanted to get my wife's attention however I could. I felt so desperate.

I wound up in the hospital, and they wanted to keep me for a two-week evaluation, but I was not really interested in anyone's help. So, when Brenda came to visit, I just got in the car with her and went home. It took some time, but I eventually accepted the fact that my life with the mother of my kids was over. It was then that everything that we had acquired in our life together did not matter to me any longer. We had been buying our house, and we had lots of toys: motorcycles; nice vehicles; and a travel trailer. Yes, we had accumulated some good material things during our time together, but then it did not matter.

After a whole lot of deceptive thinking about how to make Diane pay for hurting me, I realized that it was better just to walk away from it all, and that is exactly what I did. I just walked away and began, once again, doing the same old thing I have always done to keep my mind off my losses. It was after this, when I had determined in my mind just to give up and let everything go, that I started down a path that led me to the deepest and darkest place that I could ever imagine for anyone in this life.

While Brenda and her husband Charles were a comfort for me for the little time that I stayed in my home, they were also doing drugs. I found out they had meth in the house, and I really did not care for that at first. However, I eventually started participating, and that was a horrible choice for me to make. I did not do it all the time. I was only snorting it in the beginning; however, this quickly changed, and my use became more frequent as I started hanging around my old friends again.

During the first year of living in our home without my wife and kids, I made a solid decision

that I did not want to be there; I found it awful to be there alone in the home we had shared. I decided to move out and sell the house to Brenda and Charles. I quickly moved in with a couple of my old buddies a few miles away, and it was not long before I started hanging out at the bars and my drug use greatly increased. I did not know it at the time, but one of my buddies was deep into the meth scene. In fact, he was involved with some high rollers who had other people cooking the drugs for them. As time went on, I hung out more and more with the people that my buddy was involved with. Then, one night when we were about to go out to the bars, my buddy asked me to set him up with a shot of meth while he jumped in the shower. I had shot meth early in my life a few times, so I did what he asked. After he got out of the shower and did his shot, I decided to do one myself. That was a huge mistake. I kid you not, that shot of meth took my life from light to darkness in a matter of seconds. When I look back on it even now, the memory of it is so real that it is mind blowing. However mysteriously fun and exciting it appeared to be in the beginning, this journey to hell was slow and painful.

Let me assure you folks; it is one big plot by a masterful, deceptive serpent. Yes, he lies, and he wants to trick us into choosing a whole lot of pain and misery here on Earth in hopes to bring us to the depths of hell for our eternal home. It slowly strips away the good things God gave us in this life and sucks each of its victims dry of all the joy that comes with the blessed life God created for all to enjoy. My life as an "IV meth addict" was a battle for approximately ten years. During the first year, I was still able to function somewhat in society. As far as I knew, the only people who knew I was shooting meth were the other drug addicts who used with me.

Most of the IV drug users kept their use a secret. I eventually came to a place where I could not have cared less. Most IV users shot their drugs on an area of their body where people could not detect their needle marks. I was not one of those people. Rather, I just started wearing long sleeve shirts no matter what time of the year it was, and before I realized what was going on, I was hanging out in big time drug dealers' homes, as well as in the bars where they hung out. I came to know that there are people and places filled with the darkness of hell that can only come from the devil and his servants.

In fact, I saw things at these people's homes that would cause most people in their right mind to either throw up or pass out. It is as if the people participating in this drug scene have given into the darkness. They have made it a way of life and are living for the devil himself. Even though they have been deceived, most of them do not care. They are participating in nothing but darkness and evil. They say one thing and do another. Their whole plan is to deceive you and take whatever they can get from you. They will tell you that you are their friend but will use you as a scapegoat whenever possible. They do nothing but lie, cheat, steal, and deceive to keep others from knowing that they are living in evil.

Allow me to share a horrible experience while I was living in darkness. This dreadful scene did not affect me at the time; however, after I was clean, it truly was sickening and mind blowing to remember. I once watched this meth addict mother, with her newborn baby in her arms, struggle to inject herself with meth. She could not seem to hit her vein for like ten minutes or so. In fact, blood was running all down her arm until she finally begged her boyfriend to do her dirty work for her with her new baby in her arms!

Another time while I was lost in the meth scene, I was at a bar that was well known for the meth crowd and hosting many drug dealers. While there one evening, some people asked me if I wanted to go shoot some dope with them. Of course, I said, "Yes!", so we went right down the road from the bar to this couples' home. The man let us into the home so we could do our thing. He did his shot and went back to the bar. After I did my shot of dope, I started looking around the home. The house was a nasty mess everywhere you looked. It stank, had dirty diapers all over the place, and when I looked in the bedrooms there were little kids sleeping on a mattress on the floor. Mommy and daddy were at the bar whooping it up while their kids, as little as two or three years old, were left there in the house all by themselves.

Honestly, I have seen that in a lot of homes where mom and dad are out of their minds on meth. Meth will make you care about nothing but yourself and what brings you pleasure. There appears to be a big difference in the way a person chooses to do this drug, but most of my meth use was spent around IV users. This specific way of meth use put me in a whole different world that I had no idea existed.

I would also say that there are a whole lot of good people in this world who do not realize the darkness or wickedness that looms, most likely in their own neighborhoods. The devil and those who have given themselves over to him are very deceptive. There is a spiritual force from hell at work in our world; however, you may not be aware of it, or you may not always recognize it when you see it. But it does exist among us.

So, life went on for me, and the next seven years were a serious roller coaster ride. It consisted of a battle within me to try and forget the past by sedating myself with incredible amounts of meth. Yet, there were times during those years where I found myself hoping to get clean and to be reconciled into my family's life.

However, it was a battle I was not going to win on my own. As I was going through life without Diane and the kids, I never took anyone else's feelings into consideration. My thoughts were, "I am free to do whatever I want again, and no one is going to tell me what to do!" See, in my mind, my kids were safely tucked away at grandma and grandpa's house, and everyone else was an adult who could take care of themselves. As I began to slip further into darkness, it never dawned on me the evil that awaited me, the evil that wanted to destroy my life and soul forever.

As you read the account of my life, take into serious consideration that this evil is available to everyone who chooses it. What I am telling you is that I made a whole lot of bad choices that caused me to fall deeper into the bondage of evil that consumed my life. Yes, it awaits anyone who chooses it. I can personally testify that we will reap what we sow, just as the Bible tells us. I most certainly did.

Make no mistake: God is not mocked, for a person will reap only what he sows, because the one who sows for his flesh will reap corruption from the flesh, but the one who sows for the spirit will reap eternal life from the spirit. (Galatians 6:7-8) {NAB}

God almighty has given each of us a free will. In fact, we all know right from wrong. So, the truth is this; I have no excuse for the poor choices that led me to the deep darkness that corrupted my life.

CHAPTER 4: DEEP DARKNESS

During my first year of being single and evolving into a serious, out of control meth addict, one of my long-time buddies, Mitchell, called me and asked me if I wanted to go to work with him. Mitchell explained that the job was in San Antonio, Texas, and it would be hard work for not much pay. I had worked with Mitchell and this company, but at that time they had paid well because the work was in California. However, it did not pay the same in these other states where we would be working. This company often worked on military bases where we went in and jackhammered out huge old slabs of cement. These were the runways where airplanes taxied or parked. Then we replaced the slabs with new ones and sealed them, which was physically difficult work. So, Mitchell explained to me that we had to go do these jobs in the south if we wanted to be a part of the jobs that would be starting back in California. The job in California was going to pay around $28 an hour, but we only got $12 an hour in the other states.

Well, I was not doing anything good at the time, so I said yes. Believe me, it was better than the road I was headed down at that time, which as I found out later, would be pure agony. Our first stop was Kelly Air Force Base in San Antonio, Texas. We rented a little apartment where the cockroaches were big, and drugs were easy to find. However, the drugs available there were not what I preferred. My choice of drug was meth, and at the time it was hard to find in Texas. So instead, I spent most of my time drinking and working.

Once we were done with the Texas job, we moved on to Louisiana on the other side of the Mississippi River where we were only a few miles from New Orleans. We got to be a part of the Mardi Gras, though, we mostly stayed to ourselves while we were there. The New Orleans area has a unique darkness around it, but we were willing to stick it out, so we were sure to get on at the higher paying jobs that were coming up in California. During this time, I allowed a woman into my life from back home who would give me my last child. Laila was exceptionally beautiful, and I was lonely and hurt. I do not know if she really wanted a child or to become a mother, or if she just wanted me to take care of her.

So, in no time, I wound up with a beautiful daughter who is still a huge part of my life today. Thankfully, she has four beautiful little girls who love their grandpa a whole lot. Altogether, I had five children with four women. I am not proud of that, but I thank God for them all. I have three daughters and two sons, and twelve grandbabies. My oldest son, Paul, died, but he gave his life to Jesus on his deathbed. I know I will see him again in heaven.

Mitchell and I eventually made our way back to Sacramento from New Orleans and waited for our next job that would not be too far from home. It did not take me long to get my hands on some meth because it was everywhere in Sacramento. Laila and I stayed with my dad until it was time to start the job.

While in Texas, I had purchased some hypodermic needles because anyone can walk in and get them. But at that time, it was not possible to get needles that way in California. You had to show proof from your doctor to purchase them, and I believe it is still that way. I slowly started getting into meth again, and this time, money was not a problem for me. I was somehow able to balance out my drug addiction while we were working at this new place in Marysville, California. We were working twelve hours, seven days a week, and we were running ninety-pound jackhammers in 100 degree plus weather.

Given those circumstances, I did not have much time to run back the fifty miles to my drug connection in Sacramento. When we got off work, it was a couple of beers, some sort of fast food, a shower, and then to bed. We were working seven days a week, so we had no time off. In fact, we never got a chance to cash any checks. I only cashed one check while we were there for those three and a half months.

With all that overtime, our checks were around $2500 a week that we did not need. We had no time for anything but work, and that is what we did. I remember that when we finished, I had a whole lot of money, but that was not good for me because I was still using meth to cover up the pain of the past. I moved up in the hills with my friend who I had helped get a job so he could make some good money, too. He allowed me and Laila to live up at his house until we could find a place. He went on to the next job with that company. However, I was not willing to go because by this time I had a pocket full of money that got me lots of friends, meth, and booze.

A short time later, I found a little cabin on the other side of the highway for $250 a month. So, Laila and I moved in, and I started my journey down the road that would bring me a whole bunch of serious hell. Many people who were caught up in the meth world, and the meth itself, deceived me with lies and deceit. However, I want you to fully understand, I am the one that allowed them into my life.

This is the critical part of my story where the darkness overtook my life, and its goal was to destroy me and my family. May the God of Heaven and Earth come soon to fulfill His prophetic commitment, to one day abolish the works of the devil and all evil that brings horrible pain and suffering to people in this world.

I am telling my story so you may know how horrible the dark side is, and how incredible the Light of the world can be if you will only choose Him. Furthermore, I fell into a world that I had no idea existed; it was horrible, assiduous, evil, and from the devil. God is light and full of goodness; the devil is dark and full of lies and deception. I had no idea what I was getting myself into in the beginning. The fact was I had been completely captured by this wicked drug and its evil effects. When I look back on those first few months, it was like I was being mysteriously and dreadfully transformed into someone who would be completely useless for anything good in this life.

Moreover, I was putty in the hands of Satan. Though it all seemed harmless and fun at first, the end results were incredibly damaging to my heart, mind, and soul. It all started out as appealing and fun. It drew me into its captivating spell. It eventually blinded me and allowed the forces of darkness to overtake my life. I continued down that path for a steady two years of daily filling my veins with toxic meth, and it was physically, mentally, and spiritually damaging me. I am here to tell you that meth is straight from the depths of hell.

In addition, Satan is using this terrible drug to destroy people's lives, and his goal is to keep them from going to Heaven, securing for them a spot in eternal torment. For many months, all I wanted to do was run around from place to place getting high and meeting different people. I continually ran around every part of Sacramento, and it was mind boggling that everywhere I went, people were using meth. Moms, dads, brothers, sisters, and young kids.

I had no idea this many people in one city could be doing meth. It was crazy; it was like an epidemic. It felt like I had fallen into another dimension. A good description would be the Twilight Zone. Then one day I left Laila up at the cabin and went to Sacramento to score some more meth.

When I did this, I got caught up with the meth scene there and did not want to go back. So, she left me, but I did not care because I was totally lost on the drugs; all I could care about was getting high on meth and having sex.

A lot of nasty, horrible, and evil things are attached to drugs and alcohol. The use and abuse of them will open the door to the forces of darkness that exist among us. Eventually, all I cared about was sex and drugs. My mind was captivated by these demonic forces, and I was blind to its destructive consequences. I was hurting my family. They could see the change that was happening in my life, but my mind was blinded. There would be many trials and devastating tribulations because of my selfish choices.

It took many years of emotional stress and torment before I realized where my pain and suffering had come from. The worst of this evil that I fell into was the people who had given themselves over to the depths of the darkness. They were sold out to its deception, and Satan could use them to capture others with his evil plans. All I wanted to do was stay high and run around all night looking for people who were partying and using meth. This lifestyle eventually caught up with me, and I went to jail again for ninety days. After I sobered up in that jail, it was like I had taken a huge breath of new life. It felt so good not to be strung out and constantly running all over town to find more dope and wicked things to do. Of course, I told Laila that I was done with that lifestyle, and that I was going to be good when I got out of that jailhouse. Folks, I was not out four hours before I was right back where I had left off, shooting high powered meth that made me stupid!

Once again, it had me, and I was headed for a roller coaster ride into the darkness that I will never forget. Eventually, I was so high on meth that I could not be with Laila, who had just given birth to my beautiful daughter. Even then, I knew I was not in my right mind, and the best thing for them was for me to leave and not come back. After my they left, I really went on a binge. I had just received my retirement money from a past job. We had been living on unemployment, but now, with another large amount of money, and no one trying to tell me what I should be doing, I just went off the rails with meth.

I slipped deep into the utter darkness. With all the drugs and money, I would just get in my car and drive until I would find myself at some new place in town with new friends that were all doing meth. There were times when I would go back to my old friends and share some different kind of meth with them. Just like there's different kinds of marijuana, or heroin, there are different types of meth, and they can affect the user in different ways. For example, some of it is much more potent, and some will affect your body more than your mind.

I eventually ran out of money. I had blown most of it on drugs and partying with others. When you have a drug addiction and you run out of money, the next thing you do is start trading anything you have of value for the drug so you can stay high. I lost the vehicles I had bought with that chunk of money, either by selling them, or some other drug addict taking my stuff when I went to jail. I lost the home I was living in, too.

CHAPTER 5: MORE BAD CHOICES

I was in and out of jail for ten years. My jail time was primarily for probation violations that usually put me away for a few months at a time. Petty charges usually came with my being arrested. For example, I would be found with small amounts of drugs or drug paraphernalia. When you are out running around all night, high on drugs, you will eventually get pulled over. The cops can tell just by looking at people what a person is all about. Believe me, the police know what is happening in your neighborhood.

So, I gave up everything I had, including family and friends, for meth. The next thing I knew I was in the streets on foot with the clothes on my back and a few drug addicted friends that would put up with me. However, it did not take long to wear out my welcome. You see, if you do not have anything that may benefit these other addicts, you will not remain welcome to hang out with them anymore. The drug world declares this incredible myth that you can get to the top by being the most deceptive, lying, cheating, manipulating thief you can be. It is a world full of hate, violence, and crime. Its primary source of power comes from the devil himself whom the Bible states, "Is the father of lies." (John. 8:44 {NIV})

At this juncture in my journey, I ran around Sacramento on foot for a few months, meeting a few new people and coming across some old friends who were also on drugs. But it was long after I was on foot that I realized all my resources in Sacramento were gone. I could have gone to any of my family, but I was too ashamed to do that.

Well, one day I remembered having a conversation with an old friend. He had told me that Mitchell, the friend who had worked with me subcontracting for the military, had gotten a divorce, and was living alone up in the foothills outside of Corning, California. I distinctly remember the day I walked for miles to the on-ramp at I-5, in downtown Sacramento. I had on a t-shirt, Levi's 501 jeans, and tennis shoes, all of which had holes in them. But the holes in my shoes and clothing could not compare to the disgusting holes in my arms from the many times that I shot up meth.

But on that day, none of that mattered; I just wanted to get out of Sacramento and be free from the nightmare I was living. It was a perfect fit for both my friend and me at the time. We both needed some support to overcome the serious heartbreaks we were dealing with in our lives. After a few weeks of semi-recovery from all the meth I had been doing, it was time to get back to normal things that come with life. When a person is overcome by darkness, there is a significant amount of time involved before he can begin to enter back into the light of life that comes with God's creation. The good things in this life are available for everyone, even those who do not believe in God, even for those who feel they hate God.

"His sun shines on bad people and on good people. He sends rain on those who are right with God and on those who are not right with God." (Matthew 5:45b {NLV})

All of humanity has access to God's goodness for life; however, there will soon be a day of judgement for everyone. In the meantime, God provides good things to all. My friend had a contractor buddy who eventually put us both to work. It was part time, but it was just what we needed to support us and pay what few bills we had up there off the grid on my friend's property. Apart from the energy which was collected by his solar panels, there was no electricity for my friend's home. The cold showers were not nice, but I surely appreciated them. After being homeless for so long, soap and water were a precious gift. I did not drink much alcohol while I was strung out on meth, but I had been a beer drinker for most of my life. So, of course, that is what I immediately picked back up as I began to recover from many months of drug abuse. After a few months, I began to let my family know where I was. During the years that I was running around Sacramento strung out and off the hook, I refused to go around any of my family. So, I lived up in the hills with my friend for around a year until he went off to Alaska to work. He had not been gone a week when I did meth with some girl who asked me to take her boyfriend back home to Oregon. On the way back, I got pulled over in Yreka, California. I was not surprised to hear that I had a no-bail warrant out of Sacramento County. Eventually, I was transported to Sacramento County where the judge gave me ninety days in the county jail.

When I got out of jail, I went to my mom's home in North Highlands, California, where I immediately started looking for work. It took some doing to get my class 'A' truck driver's license back; I had to finish my DUI classes first, which consisted of twelve months of weekly classes, but I did it. My old boss let me work on the dock until I got my Class 'A' back. So, I then had the job I had been doing most of my life, and of course, I was still drinking. The only thing missing from my usual lifestyle was a woman.

Let me bring some clarity to how I lived most of my adult life. I was a control freak when it came to my life and my women. It was my way or no way. It was really that simple for me. None of it was easy on the women in my life because I was a horrible verbal abuser like my dad. I controlled women with fear, but I used deceptive charm. Most of the time, I only had to use words to control them.

It was not long before I found myself in a relationship that would be explosive and damaging for everyone involved. It lasted for only a few years because of the usual turmoil that I brought to the relationship. My excessive drinking, which always led me back to the dope, created a vicious cycle that I thought I would never be able to overcome. Around 1999-2001, I started struggling with the most staggering battles of all my life. Every day when I woke up it was all I could do to try and stay clean. At the time, my dad and his girlfriend Lilly were living out in the country in a big old house with property behind it. They had a 5th wheel trailer which they rented to me. Around 2000, I was doing pretty good with staying off the meth, though I was still slipping every now and then. I was also still struggling with maintaining a steady job, but somehow, I would always bounce back and get another one.

Getting another job trucking was not hard to do with a fully endorsed truck driver's license. My problem was staying away from the meth so I could show up for work. One day I happened to run into Mickey, a friend from my past who was then living in the little town where I was staying. Mickey asked me to stop by and see him some time, so I did. Come to find out, he was caught up into the meth scene, big time! Well, little by little, I found myself shooting meth again, and to my surprise, so was he.

CHAPTER 6: ROCK BOTTOM

This started my very last journey of meth use. It really got me that time. It was not long before I lost my job and once again gave up everything I had for my addiction to meth. Through my worst days, my dad was really the only one who never stopped trying to help me. It was around my fortieth birthday, and he decided he would have a little birthday party for me. So, he invited my family members over to his house. He could see I was depressed and struggling with my addictions. A few of my family members came, and it lifted my spirit a little bit. I even got a few gifts. Surprisingly, my oldest sister Cathy gave me the one thing I thought no one would ever give me... a book.

The book was Left Behind, by Tim Lahaye and Jerry B Jenkins. To my surprise, I started reading it. I later recognized that what was in that book was exactly what I needed to hear in that gloomy time of my life. It was about the second coming of the Lord and the rapture of His church. It is a fictional story written about the end times prophesied in the Bible. That book got me really thinking about where I was going to go when my life was over. Around this time in my life, I started picking up the Bible to read, but I also started using again, and eventually, I came to the place where I could not function in the real world any longer. Because of the excessive drug use, I fell into a deep dark place that was incredibly frightening.

I started isolating myself, and there were times when I felt the presence of the dark side like no other time in my meth addiction. What I realize now is that at that time there was a war being waged in the spiritual realm, a battle for my soul. There were times when I felt that the evil and demonic presence in my life was on the verge of winning my soul, and I started slipping deeper into the darkness with the idea of killing myself with meth. I started getting different types of meth from different sources, and I was using it in every way possible: shooting it, smoking it, drinking it, snorting it.

This went on for three to four months; I could feel nothing. I came to a place where I realized I was dead inside, and I realized I could not have feelings for anything, or anyone. It was the most terrifying place I have ever been in my life. I knew no one could help me, not my mother or father; no counseling, nor any medical treatment from anyone could help.

Eventually, I came to a place in my life where I knew there was only One who could help me in my dim, dark, miserable situation, God. So, I did what needed to be done. I began earnestly crying out to God for help. I remember a day, sometime in early 2000, when I was just totally wiped out on meth, and my mom and dad decided to invite me to the church they were attending. I believe my dad had just started going back to church after many years of dropping out. My thoughts have always been, he was not just doing it for himself. The night before that Sunday in 2000, I was really being tormented by the demons I had allowed back into my life through the excessive use of toxic methamphetamines.

I could feel the presence of evil so strongly that I could not stay in my trailer, but I was

determined to make that church service the next day, no matter what I had to do. I got in my truck and drove across town to my mom's and tried to rest until the morning. I remember lying on my mom's sofa watching TV, experiencing and seeing things that were not of this realm. I know now that the power that overtook my mind that night was from the power of Satan. I thought I was going to die that night or lose my mind. I lay there until morning, and then made my way back to my dad's place. Together, we made our way to that big church. There had to be 800-900 people there that day; however, that did not matter to me. I was in such mental agony, and I just wanted it to go away. My faith that day was completely in God, and that faith was incredibly strong. I completely believed that the Lord was going to deliver me from the evil that had overtaken my life that day. I sat through that service expecting God to do something miraculous, and even to the very end of that service, my faith did not waver. I knew there would be an altar call. So, when they invited people to the altar for prayer, I went down. My mom and one of the pastors were waiting for me there.

At the altar, they anointed my head with holy oil. Immediately, a loud scream came out of me, and I went out like a light. I remember now that as I lay on the floor in peace, I thought they were going to wake me up, and I did not want to get up and face life again. However, they reached down and brought me to my feet. I remember that another pastor came running from the other side of the altar to see what had happened. The incredibly loud scream that had come out of me had drawn the attention of the whole church. I did not understand at the time how I could have gone so quickly from serious mental turmoil to a peace that would eventually change my life forever.

While I was reading my Bible sometime later, that peace that I could not understand was confirmed by God's Word.

"Then Philip went down to the city of Samaria and preached Christ to them. And the multitudes with one accord heeded the things spoken by Philip, hearing and seeing the miracles which he did. For unclean spirits, crying with a loud voice, came out of many who were possessed; and many who were paralyzed, and lame were healed. [8]And there was great joy in that city." (Acts.8:5-8 {NKJV}).

I know now that the Lord had miraculously healed me and delivered me from the evil that had overtaken my life.

Unfortunately, this was not yet the end of my battle with meth. Nor was it the end of the battle for my soul, but after my experience at the church, my faith and hope in God was much stronger than ever before. I stayed clean for a few months but fell back into the devil's trap once again. It was not long before my mental anguish retuned. I can recall one night when there was a group of people out front at my dad's place. I could not be around them because my mind was so exhausted from the many battles I had experienced with the meth.

Then, I heard this encouraging voice loud and clear tell me to go to my sister's house for help. This was Cathy, who had given me the Left Behind book. So, I made my way there, and thankfully, Cathy and her husband Wade allowed me in. They knew exactly what I had been going through. My little brother, Keith, lived with my sister and her husband, and they were all very involved at a Pentecostal church and believed in the healing power of God.

I asked them if they would help me, and so they took me into the living room and asked me to get on my knees. I did as they asked, and they anointed my head with oil and started laying their hands on me and praying in the Spirit, or what is better known as tongues. They instructed me to cry out to Jesus, which I did very quietly. They continued to pray and encouraged me to cry out louder, and I did. I eventually cried out from the depths of my soul, and I immediately started speaking in tongues. It was just like that day in Phoenix, Oregon, when I was a little boy. But this time it was tongues of fire that came with incredible life changing power that would change me forever!

Listen to me folks, I assure you that whatever your trials or tribulations may be in this life, know this; if you will humble yourselves and sincerely cry out to the Lord Jesus and believe that He is the only one that can help you, it will be done for you. I wish I could tell you that this was

the end of my trials and tribulations, but that was not the case. However, things were changing. The Lord finally had me going in the right direction, but my mind was still in need of healing from the many years of porn addiction, meth, and alcohol abuse. My heart and mind

were in desperate need of God's restorative power which takes time and effort on the part of anyone seeking deliverance from the powerful effects of sin.

So, I started going to church, and I was trying extremely hard to give up my offensive and destructive ways; they had ruled my life for many years. I also went back to work driving a truck. It appeared that everything in my life now was going to be alright. I was reading the Bible and praying; I no longer had the desire to drink, do drugs, or use foul language. This was huge for me, and I could see real change taking place in my life. People could see that I was really trying to change my life. Most importantly, God and my family could see it.

I was still not healed in my mind from the many years of substance abuse; however, I know now, after all those years of abuse, that my mind needed to be renewed by the Word of God. Now I know that to be set free takes time, determination, devotion and dedication to the Lord and His truth. When a person genuinely wants a new life, and relief from their pain, suffering, and worldly sorrows, they must put their faith in the God that created them.

"Then they cried out to the LORD in their trouble, and He saved them out of their distresses. He sent His word and healed them and delivered them from their destructions." (Psalm 107:19-20 {NKJV})

Though I was in the process of getting my life back together, the many years of meth use and the horrible demonic influences that damaged my mind could not be erased easily. I remember nights when I would be waiting in my work truck for my number to be called so I could go to the docks and get my truck unloaded. I would read my Bible, then think about the new life the Lord was giving me. Of course, I would also think about the problems from my past. I did not realize at the time that I had to leave my old life behind, including the woman that I was with at the time. This relationship had always been a terrible mess, and it was undeniably the fault of us both. The relationship was still bringing a great deal of stress into my life, and it kept my mind going back and forth with thoughts of good and evil. This went on for about three or four months, and these crazy thoughts from the past were haunting me. I would hear voices telling me that certain people were evil, and that God wanted me to kill them. I want to make something absolutely clear to all who are reading this: God will never tell you to kill or harm anyone. God is a God of love and truth! Today I know my mind was still damaged and was still recovering from my past abuse.

I pressed on daily, struggling with horrible thoughts, hoping, and praying for them to go away. More than anything, I wanted the peace of God to overtake my heart and mind. I did not realize that it would take a couple of years of sobriety for that to take place. You see, after many years of substance abuse, there needs to be a time of restoration and recovery for a person's mind to become clear and stable. As I continued to try and live a new and better life while fighting daily mental battles, I eventually gave in to those voices and committed a horrible crime that devastated me and my family.

CHAPTER 7: JESUS, THE LIGHT OF MY LIFE

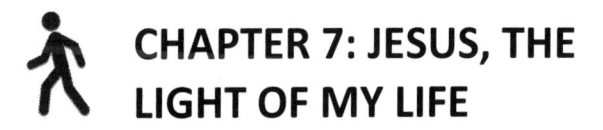

Every morning when I wake up, I thank God that no one died as a result my actions during the many years I was living in addiction. My addiction led me to do terrible things that brought a huge number of problems into my life, and into the lives of those I love. I wound up in the Sacramento County jail, looking at a possible life sentence. It was while I was in the jail that I finally made the best choice of my life. I got on my knees next to my bunk, and I cried out to Jesus, asking Him sincerely from the depths of my heart to save me.

I had many things to recover from that that had harmed not only me, but my family as well. My recovery journey would be hard, but in the end, it is one of the most rewarding times of my life. I was locked up in the Sacramento County jail for two years, where I spent most of my time reading the Bible, praying, and getting to know the One who had saved me. He was in the process of healing me and giving me a new life, and even though I was looking at a possible life sentence, it was in that jailhouse that I learned how to put my faith in God.

I was locked up in my cell twenty-two hours a day, so I had lots of time to read my Bible and pray. One day when I had been there about eight months, I was on my knees praying, and a light came on inside me. In that moment I knew that I was truly saved and on my way to Heaven, and I knew that everything I was reading in the Bible was true. I could not deny that Jesus was real and was now living inside of me.

The love of God overtook my life, and all I wanted to do from that point on was to honor Him with the rest of my life, no matter where I had to go to do it. After learning that the Lord was in complete control of all of my life and my destiny, I surrendered to Him. That is the day His peace began to settle my mind and the real healing and restoration began for me. I was not fighting my case; I just put it all at the foot of His throne and trusted Him. "Let us then approach God's throne of grace with confidence, so that we may receive mercy and find grace to help us in our time of need." (Hebrews.4:16 {NIV})

Each day I simply went about doing God's business, leaving everything up to Him, because all my faith was in Him.

I had many different cell mates while I was in that jail cell, but the most significant one was a young Russian man, Victor, who was looking at two murder charges. However, Victor told me he did not do this crime. Every time we got out of our cell, he would have a Bible study, or he would be praying with others and encouraging them to put their trust in Jesus. I was always there ready and willing to learn more. Victor's dad was a well-known pastor in the Russian community of Sacramento. Apparently, he grew up in the church. He had strayed from the Lord and started hanging out with the wrong people, and of course, started making poor choices for his life, finding himself in a lot of trouble. After being locked up, Victor repented and renewed his relationship with the Lord. He taught me how to press into the Word of God. After a few months, he told me his time was up in Sacramento County jail because he had won his case. Victor was eventually going to be transferred to another county to fight another murder case which he eventually won as well.

One day, before he left, Victor told me he had been praying for someone to continue to do Bible study in our cell block because they were moving him soon. He said, "The Lord has chosen you, Bubby." I did not know the Bible that well, but I was willing to do whatever the Lord wanted, so I stayed right on track with our Bible study after he left. It was amazing how many guys would come to hear the Word of God, and they came every time I went to the table to share.

I soon became known as the man of God, because everywhere I would go, I would be talking about the Bible or be praying with people, encouraging them to put their trust in Jesus. I shared the love of Jesus with men who were looking to go away for life because of their many poor choices. A personal relationship with the Lord can bring great comfort no matter what your circumstances are in this life.

The Lord is waiting for all to come to Him in time of need. No matter how bad your situation may be, Jesus wants to help you. Here is what the Lord showed me after a year and half in the jail. First, He showed me that I was forgiven for all the bad I had done, and that before giving Him control, my life had been all wrong. I had been living a lie, and now He was going to show me how to live by His truth. Jesus answered, I am the way the truth and the life. (John 14: 6 {NIV}) When I got that revelation deep in my heart, I knew that I had to live it out every day of my life.

After almost two years, and many evaluations by psychologists and psychiatrists, I finally got a trial date. The first time we met, I told my attorney that I was going to tell the truth no matter what might happen. He was able to work out a deal with the district attorney. The deal was a twelve-year sentence with a sanity trial to see if we could prove that I was not in my right mind when I committed the crime. I took that deal.

We got to take my case before a judge without a jury. If we could prove to the judge that I was not in my right mind when I committed the crime, I would not have to do the twelve years in prison. For three and half months, the prosecution insisted that I was sane when I committed the crime. I, on the other hand, told the truth because by this time in my relationship with the Lord, I knew wherever the truth is, Jesus is there!

At the end of the trial, the judge looked at the court and said, "I believe there was no malingering in Mr. Wallace," which means I was not faking a mental illness to get out of the consequences of the crime that I had committed. The judge believed I was telling the truth. Remember, Then you will know the truth, and the truth will set you free! (John 8:32 {NIV}) When the judge gave the verdict after three and half months of trial, I gave all the glory to God. With my own eyes, I watched God do a miracle in that judge's heart. It was even more amazing when the Lord confirmed it by His Word.

"The king's heart is in the hand of the LORD, Like the rivers of water; He turns it wherever He wishes." (Proverbs 21:1 {NKJV})

Well, I did not go free, but instead of twelve years in prison, I was sent to a state hospital. Thank you, Jesus! I was to be locked up for at least five years. I am so thankful I did not have to go to prison. I took those years separated from the outside world and focused on my relationship with the Lord. The hospital could have held me for life; it all depended on my behavior. I just followed the rules and lived my life for the Lord, and miraculously, I was out in three years.

When I got out, I had to live in a transitional home and go to outpatient programs. For me, it was a new start with a new life back out in the world. I had rules to follow to continue to be free. After looking at my criminal history, most of the doctors diagnosed me with antisocial behavior, which means I did not care for rules. Most of my life, I did whatever I wanted and did not care about the consequences. However, I knew that Jesus had given me a new life, and I was now to live it according to His truth with peace and love.

Jesus changed my heart so that I could then truly care about others and show them that the love of God can change anyone, even me. After five years of allowing the Lord to do a work inside of me, all I wanted to do was serve Him.

When I was locked up, I knew I wanted to go to Bible college and become a pastor so that I could help others who were bound by the lies of the devil. I was on a short leash with my outpatient program, but after about a year, they allowed me to pursue my dream. The first thing I had to do was get fifty dollars for the application at the Bible college. The home I was living in was not far from the American River which has a bike trail that runs for miles through Sacramento.

I had a bicycle, so I grabbed some plastic garbage bags and rode my bike to a part of the river where I knew there would be lots of people putting in their rafts to float down the river. I could not believe it when I got there. The garbage cans in the park were overflowing with cans, mostly beer cans. I like to tell people the devil helped me get into Bible college with all those beer cans because I cashed them in to pay my application fee. However, I knew it was a gift from God. He was the one who put the idea on my heart in the first place. It was a gold mine to me; God truly works in mysterious ways! Well, it was just another sign to me that the Lord was in control and was leading me down the path that would fulfill that dream of getting a Bible education and becoming a pastor.

But before I could qualify for grant money, I had to get my G.E.D. Though I had taken care of most of that while I was locked up, I went to a school where they helped me study for and pass the math portion. Not only did they help me prepare, but the course was tuition free. It was hard for me to jump over all those hurdles to get to the place of fulfilling my dream, but let me tell you, I would not have been able to accomplish any of it without the Lord. The Bible says, "Trust in the LORD with all your heart and lean not on your own understanding; ⁶In all your ways acknowledge Him, and He shall direct your paths." (Proverbs 3:5-6 {NKJV})

God showed me great favor at the Bible college. At first, I was getting money from the federal government to pay for classes, but after a few months of school, I was told that if I wanted to get a degree, I was going to need more money than what I was already receiving. So, I met with the financial guy, and he said I could try to get money from the Cal-Grant program, which is free money from the state of California for those who qualify. Because I had not graduated from high school, he did not think I would qualify; however, he said, "Let's fill out the paperwork, pray, send it in, and trust the Lord." A few months later, I got something in the mail from the Cal-Grant people, but I did not understand it, so I took it to the financial guy at the school. He took it out of the envelope and after reading it he yelled,

"Hallelujah! You have been granted the largest amount they give out!" I was only planning on getting my associate degree, but with all the money they gave me, I went ahead and got my bachelor's degree as well. It took me seven years to get a four-year degree.

Ultimately, here is what you need to know: I never went to one day of high school, yet I graduated from college with honors. So, while I was a very busy man working on this awesome dream God put in my heart to one day be a pastor and be able to help others come to the saving knowledge of God's truth and grace, there were still things from my past that needed to be mended. My family was deeply affected by my many years of alcohol and drug abuse, and I was not sure if healing was even possible, but God had a plan.

CHAPTER 8: RECOVERING FROM THE DARKNESS

Before I got out of the hospital, I was told that I would have to be in a recovery program, that it was a part of the conditions of my release. So, I started praying for a Christian twelve-step program. I had heard they existed, but I did not know what they were called or if there were any in the Sacramento area. And so, I prayed that when I got out, the Lord would lead me to a Christian twelve-step program. While living in the transitional home, I was told I had to go to certain groups required by my outpatient program. They were provided, and though they did not have any recovery groups, they gave us a list of recovery programs in our area of Sacramento. Fortunately for me, I found a Christian recovery program right down the street from my transitional home. I used to take walks in the area, and I would pass by this little church and wonder what kind of church it was. I was really drawn to it, so one day I went to check it out. A very polite elderly secretary greeted me and then showed me around the church.

I learned that her name was Grace, and after she had showed me around and I headed to the door, she said, "Wait a minute...we have just started a recovery program. Do you think you might be interested? It is called 'Celebrate Recovery.'" It was exactly what I had been praying for, a Christian twelve-step recovery program. You see, I had been to all the secular ones while I was locked up, and I did not care for them. To be honest, I was only joining the group because I was required to go, and it would get me out of the house for a while, but I was excited to begin.

I remember after a few meetings, some of the men told me that there was going to be another part of the program called "The

Step Study" which would be held on a different night. They informed me that I would need to buy some books, get a sponsor, and get an accountability partner as well. So, I agreed because the additional meeting got me out of the house one more night of the week. Well, I was in for the surprise of my life because this Step Study requires a very personal inventory of your hurts, habits, and hang-ups, present and past.

My friends from the group informed me that when we got to the fourth step, we would search our hearts, and then write down those things that had caused damage to our lives or to the lives of others. This is called an inventory. When the inventory was finished, I would make an appointment with my sponsor and "confess" the faults, failures, hurts, or sins that interfered with my recovery.

Though it was very hard to look at my past, put it all down on paper, and confess it to someone, it was one of the most rewarding and powerful healing experiences of my journey. In my first Step Study, the Lord revealed to me the root of my anger toward every woman with whom I had ever had a serious relationship. The day I shared my deepest hurts with my sponsor as he prayed for me to be healed from my past was miraculous. The Bible says, Confess your sins to each other and pray for each other so God can heal you. When a believing person prays, great things happen. (James 5:16 {NCV})

Celebrate Recovery is based on the Word of God. I am here to tell you that if you will do what the Word of God says, God Almighty will surely fulfill His promises and heal you. Because I was willing to do the work through Celebrate Recovery and trust what the Word of God told me, I was miraculously healed. My first Step Study seemed complete to me; I had been incredibly healed of serious past hurts, but the Lord wanted to restore all my relationships with those I had hurt through the many dark years of substance abuse. Therefore, I immediately went through another Step Study because I knew it was a part of God's plan for my life.

I spent around eight months setting up appointments with each member of my family. My mother, father, brothers, sisters, children, ex-wives, ex-in-laws, any and all who were a part of my life, who I knew truly loved me and were hurt by my actions. As a result of making many amends that were sometimes terribly hard and painful, I experienced another incredible miracle of the Lord. God brought amazing healing to all those broken relationships. Believe me when I tell you it did not just happen overnight. For example, at my ex-wife's appointment, I got on my knees in tears and asked her to forgive me. Today, after many years of honest friendship with her, allowing her to see the new man the Lord has made in me, we are able to live at peace with one another. In fact, I have a key to her house, and that my friends, is the hand of God. He can bring healing to anyone, no matter how badly you have messed up in this life. Listen to what I am saying folks, If you are honestly willing to do the work, God can do a work in you and all your relationships...no matter how broken they may be! The Lord wants you to have healthy relationships that come with love, trust, peace, and truth. It is a part of God Almighty's process when you surrender to His will. He wants to drive out the darkness that has corrupted us and our lives, that has deceived us and led us down paths of destruction.

CHAPTER 9: LIVING IN THE LIGHT

Permit me, please, to simply shed some light on the saving grace of Jesus Christ. He wants everyone to go to Heaven, but you must first surrender to Him. He wants to save you from the lie of the devil, and He genuinely wants you to be with Him forever in paradise. The devil wants to destroy you and deceive you; Jesus wants to save you from Satan and hell. It does not matter where you are right now; it does not matter how badly you have messed up in this life. The Lord wants you to come to Him and trust Him so that He can start you on your journey to Heaven.

The Bible is clear that there is no other way to Heaven except through Jesus. You must sincerely believe He died for your sin on the cross, and then tell someone you believe. If you declare with your mouth,

"Jesus is Lord," and if you believe in your heart that God raised Jesus from the dead, you will be saved. We believe with our hearts, and so we are made right with God. And we declare with our mouths that we believe, and so we are saved. (Romans.10:9-10{NCV})

If you are not already a child of God, allow me to lead you to the first step necessary to begin your journey to Heaven and become a child of God. Read this prayer with sincerity and begin allowing God to shine His light in you and drive out the darkness that has brought pain and suffering into your life.

"Lord Jesus, I am sorry for my sin. I am willing to turn from my sin. I receive You now as my Lord and Savior. Seal me with Your Holy Spirit for eternity and take away the blindness Satan has placed on my mind, so that I may shine as a light in this dark world for you, Jesus."

If you prayed that prayer and truly meant it, I welcome you now into the Kingdom of

God and His righteousness. I want to assure you that you are now a work in progress, and for your new life to continue to be filled with the transforming power of God, you must start reading your Bible and pray to the Lord daily. Then find some other Christians to fellowship with and go find a good solid mainline Christian church and Bible study. This is how you will continue to grow strong and stay separated from the dark things of this world.

I am a testimony of the lifesaving, life-changing power of God. I have been out of trouble for twenty years now. There are no more jails, institutions, or problems like those that had grieved me and my family in the past. During my time back out in the free world, I have continued to trust the Lord with my life. Nevertheless, it was not all peaches and cream, my friends. There have been a lot of issues from my broken past, and I needed to take care of things like child support, and my driver's license; the list was a long one.

God Almighty is in the restoration business, and He is waiting for you to come to Him no

matter how bad your life has become. No matter what your address is, He loves you and wants to be a part of your life now and forever. We have all been given free will, and the Lord will not force you to love Him. You must choose Him if you want His favor in this life, not to mention that He is your ticket to Heaven for the next! There are only two choices for the next life; one is Heaven, and the other is hell. It is your choice. You must choose your destination while you are alive in this life. Once you pass into the next life, there is no option to change your choice; it becomes permanent.

Consider what I am sharing with you friends. I just want you to know the truth. I do not want anything from you, except to see you in Heaven one day. Here is another reason why I continue to trust Jesus with my life. The conditions of my release back into society came with rules. If I had messed up or gone back to my old ways while I was in the state outpatient program, I would have been sent back to the hospital. If that had happened, the state hospital could have held me for life. Living in our society comes with rules, and these rules have a purpose. They are there for our safety. So, realizing this and knowing I was a changed man, I determined in my heart to do good and put everything in prayer to the Lord.

After about three years in the outpatient program, I went back to court to see if I could be released from the program. Fortunately for me, I was able to get all kinds of recommendation letters from many people who knew only the new man. These were the people in my church, students at the Bible college, and even the employees who supervised the program I attended. None of those people had ever met the old man, but they had heard stories about the old man.

Thankfully, they were able to sincerely testify that I was truly a changed man. It was proof to the judge that my life had changed, and I was now a responsible citizen doing well back in society.

I was now a free man again with no more restraints on my life. I had a wide-open path to do some good with my life, to give back to society, to help others find the Light of life that changed me forever. Listen, I knew that I had been saved from the darkness, and I had a great deal of the Light in my future. I found a good church, and then I got a job there. At that time, the Lord directed me to start working on my unhealthy behavior toward women.

In obeying Him in this, I joined a singles group so I could learn how to be the new man around women, a man who could care about others. I knew I was going to be a pastor and that I was going to need a godly woman by my side to help me. I needed to know how to be a godly man so I could become a godly husband. After two years of living on the south side of Sacramento, I was offered a ministry position at a Foursquare church in Rocklin, California, just north of Sacramento, and it was a divine appointment, folks.

The pastor of the church had a little ministry house next to the church; the pastor wanted me to be the men's ministry director, discipling men who were struggling with life issues. I thought it was right up my alley, and I moved into the little house. We began to fix it up for ministry. I was still in Bible college and had lots of homework to do, but I was excited for this new opportunity to help others recover from poor life choices.

I jumped headfirst into my new position at the church. My job was to disciple the men in the home as we took care of the four church facilities and worked on our recovery.

The men were required to attend church, plus do the work of keeping all the facilities clean and ready for ministry. The church had a Celebrate Recovery Ministry; in fact, that is how I wound up there. I was invited to give my testimony, and when I did, I laid eyes on the woman God had intended for me.

The pastor's vision for me and the ministry house lasted about two years, and we helped some men get their lives in order. However, as time went on, and I became a licensed minister, I still knew I needed a godly woman by my side. I became friends with a woman who was serving at the church and with Celebrate Recovery. Her name was Elaine; I was attracted to her, and I eventually realized that I wanted to get serious about her. So, I asked her if we could get to know each other on a more personal basis.

After a brief time of getting to know each other better, I presented Elaine with an offer. I told her that I wanted to court her for marriage. However, she needed to be sure that she could pour out her life for Jesus, because that was my plan for my life. My prayers for a wife always included three characteristics: that she would be a godly woman, that she would be filled with the spirit, and that she would be willing to pour out her life for Jesus.

Well, she agreed that she would pray and search her heart to see if that is what she wanted for her life. This was right around the time that Elaine and the rest of the recovery ministry team were headed to the Celebrate Recovery Summit where all kinds of Celebrate Recovery teams gather for an annual meeting at Rick Warren's church in Lake Forest, CA. The first night Rick Warren spoke, he talked about pouring out your life for Jesus.

Elaine explained to me that she was deeply touched by the message and knew that it was what the Lord wanted for her. She called me and told me she was willing to pour out her life for Jesus alongside me. Then I went to my pastor and told him that I needed a wife and that we would do the work at the church. He asked, "Who do you have in mind?" He knew my intended very well as Elaine had been there at the church for ten years. It all turned out to be another awesome divine appointment from God. I have learned through God's amazing grace that the Lord knows exactly what we need to live a good life.

He takes care of those who are willing to honor Him with their lives. This is my life scripture because God has shown me that He is alive and well and in control of all things, For it is God who works in you to will and to act in order to fulfill his good purpose. (Philippians. 2:13 {NIV})

It is fortunate that my wife loves the Lord with all her heart because after we got married, I wanted Elaine to start Bible college. She was not too excited about that. She told me she had barely made it through high school, and she did not think she was going to be able to manage earning a college education.

As a result of her willingness, the Lord did a powerful work in my beautiful wife, Elaine. She surpassed every expectation and graduated with honors, earning an associate degree in biblical counseling. She is an awesome woman of God, and I love her. I can care for her knowing she is a gift from God. We are now both ordained ministers, working at a Bible college where we see people being transformed every day into solid men and women of God. We are not perfect but have worked for many years to overcome the pain and suffering that came with living lives of drug and alcohol abuse, and adulterous relationships that brought horrible darkness into our lives.

Please allow me to share a few particularly important things that I know will help anybody that is willing to apply the truth from the Bible to their lives and begin to honestly work on recovering from their sinful past.

1. A Bible education will give you the wisdom, knowledge, and strength to overcome the adversity that comes with living in this falling world.

2. Celebrate Recovery will help you recover from the darkness and the hurts, habits, and hang-ups that brought pain and suffering into your life.

3. You must truly believe that the Bible is a love letter from God to you.

4. The Bible is the map, guide, and personal instruction that will direct you to Heaven.

My personal take on a Bible education is that there is not enough money in the world to buy back the amazing inner strength that came with learning, in-depth, the Word of God. I think everyone who gives their life to Jesus should go to Bible college. If a person genuinely wants to recover from a sinful past, I recommend Celebrate Recovery because it is founded on the Word of God.

There is nothing upon this earth that will provide for you the healing, delivering power that comes with trusting what God promises in His Word. I am amazed by how people think that God Almighty cannot simply write a book that prepares us to know Him, understand Him, and have a personal relationship with Him. He is God, the Creator, He is the One who made us and the earth, so we may enjoy Him and the good things that come with life. All He asks is that we believe what He tells us in His Word, so that He can bless us with the Light of Life.

There is great power, peace, and His provision when we live as He asks us to live.

Are you ready to see God's mercy and grace that comes to those who believe? Then, I suggest you pick up the Bible and start your journey today, so that God can start effectively working in your life. It is how your conversion begins.

For this reason, we also thank God without ceasing, because when you received the word of God which you heard from us, you welcomed it not as the word of men, but as it is in truth, the word of God, which also effectively works in you who believe. (1 Thessalonians 2:13 {NKJV})

You may believe that men wrote the Bible, but that is a mistake. Our faith must be in God, my friend. The Lord is easily wiser and more powerful than any man. Remember God is the One that has created our extremely complicated bodies. He designed us with free will, as well, so you can believe Him who is greater than all. He wants us to put our faith in Him, to put our trust in

Him. If you want to be someone who can overcome adversity in this dark and wicked world, you must put your faith in Jesus.

Listen friends, I lived for forty years on my own selfish thinking, and it brought me nothing but trouble. Not just trouble for me, but for all my loved ones. I have lived now with my faith in Jesus Christ for twenty years, and His peace that surpasses all understanding is available to me always. I do not have a bunch of serious problem in my life anymore. Sure, living this life comes with problems, but if you put your faith in Jesus, He will always be there for you no matter what you may have to go through.

Without our faith in Jesus, we will be openly affected by the devil and his destructive attacks for our lives. Jesus tells us in the Bible that the devil is a thief. He wants to rob us of the good things in the life God planned for us. Jesus wants us to live this life with His complete provision.

A thief comes to steal and kill and destroy, but I came to give life—life in all its fullness. (John. 10:10 {NCV})

Fortunately for me, I am totally convinced that God can do what He says according to His Word. I know I am forgiven and on my way to Heaven. I fully understand that there is a heaven and a hell. I know that this life comes with the light from Heaven and the darkness from hell...that we must choose wisely the paths for our lives. Many things in my life became broken because of the darkness I allowed in my life. Here is what I want you to know: Every person that is alive upon this earth comes from God. He is the Giver of life. Therefore, it is our choice to make it good or bad.

If we choose to live in darkness, it will bring into our lives the deception and destruction that the devil has planned for those who follow him. If we choose to walk in the Light, we will have the good things of life that God has planned for His followers.

Jesus tells us in John. 8:12, I am the light of the world. He who follows me shall not walk-in darkness but have the light of life {NKJV}.

I know that Jesus is the best choice I ever made. He has forgiven me of all the bad things I have ever done, and He has given me a new life that comes with love, peace, and joy!

Forgiveness

*I have been forgiven
For my sins upon this earth.
The Lord has forgiven me,
Now I know what my life is worth.*

*Jesus took me by the hand
And led me from the path of sin.
He filled me with his love
And made me whole within.*

*No longer do I grieve;
Today I have peace and joy.
Jesus has given me a new life
that no one can destroy.*

Bubby Wallace, 2006

ABOUT THE AUTHOR

Bubby Wallace is a Licensed, Ordained Minister with the Foursquare Denomination. Recovery is a passion, helping others is a gift, and Jesus is his Life. He and his wife, Elaine, currently reside in Elverta, CA.

Made in the USA
Columbia, SC
29 April 2023